Crystal Clear

Answer to Prayer

Written and Illustrated By
Jennifer S. Lyons, PMHNP

WestBow Press books may be ordered through booksellers or by contacting:

WestBow Press
A Division of Thomas Nelson & Zondervan
1663 Liberty Drive
Bloomington, IN 47403
www.westbowpress.com
844-714-3454

Written and Illustrated By Jennifer S. Lyons, PMHNP

ISBN: 978-1-6642-3316-4 (sc)
ISBN: 978-1-6642-3315-7 (hc)
ISBN: 978-1-6642-3317-1 (e)

Library of Congress Control Number: 2021908742

Print information available on the last page.

WestBow Press rev. date: 05/26/2021

This book is dedicated to Jesus Christ, the love of my life and my inspiration. He is the same yesterday today and forever. This book is also dedicated to Harold and Haley, two of my most precious blessings from Him. I love you the same yesterday, today and forever.

The brakes squeal, as the Dodge blue Shadow comes
to an abrupt stop. Gears slightly grind together, then
a faint whining is heard as the car slowly backs up.

Parking her car along an old country road, Haley and Harold's mom gets out and picks up a large painted shell turtle in the middle of the road.

Not wanting the turtle to become roadkill,

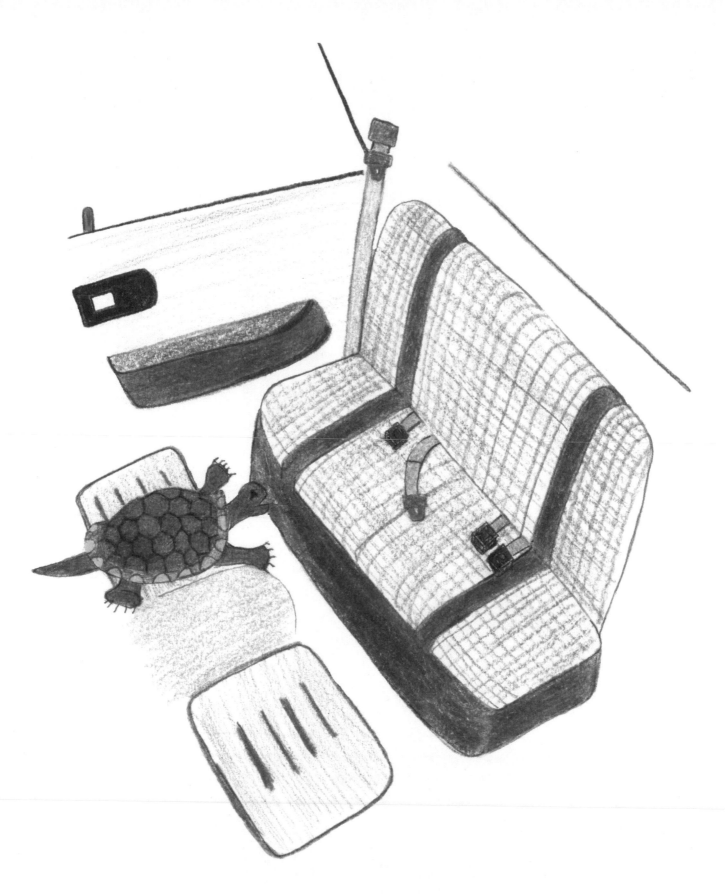

she puts it on the floor behind the passenger seat where she can keep a close eye on it and drives off toward home.

Haley and Harold arrive home from school, they are excited to meet their new pet. "What will we feed it?" asks Harold inquisitively.

"Where did you find him? Is it a boy or a girl? What will we name him?"

The list of Harold's questions
is infinite, and his blue eyes
are as seas of wonder.

"He looks lonely in there," said Haley compassionately.
"I want to find a friend for him."

"I read a book about turtles in the school library.
They eat crickets, worms, minnows, and crayfish,
she wrinkled her nose, and live bugs!"

"You have to wash your hands after you touch it because turtles carry the bacteria called sam-an-ella."

"Sam and who?" asks Haley's younger brother Harold.

Mom answers, "Salmonella. It is the same thing people get when they eat old rotten chicken." Harold makes a quirky face and contemplates weather he should touch the turtle or not.

It's ok," mom assures him. "You just have to wash your hands as a precaution for when you eat, or if you accidentally put your fingers in your mouth."

They watch intently while the enormous turtle swims around in their turtle shell sandbox filled with water. Then Haley comes up with an idea, "Come on Harold. Let's go find some rocks for him to climb on and something for him to eat."

Returning to the sandbox, Harold has a name picked out for his shiny-shelled pet. "Raphael, we will call him Raphael," as he pulls a handful of slimy worms from his denim-jeans pocket.

The search is on! The first day: worms and crickets are only appetizers. The neighbors donate a large vacant fish tank from the treasuries of their basement. It becomes a corporate neighborhood project to keep Raphael fed.

Minnows, insects, and worms from all over the neighborhood are donated. The fish tank supply is depleted all around the block. All the while Haley searches high and low for Raphael's new companion.

Off to the pet store! Haley wants to go to the pet store for some food for Raphael, some fancy fish tank rocks, and a fish net to catch some minnows in their favorite creek. One hundred grub worms and fifty minnows, that ought to be enough! Wrong!

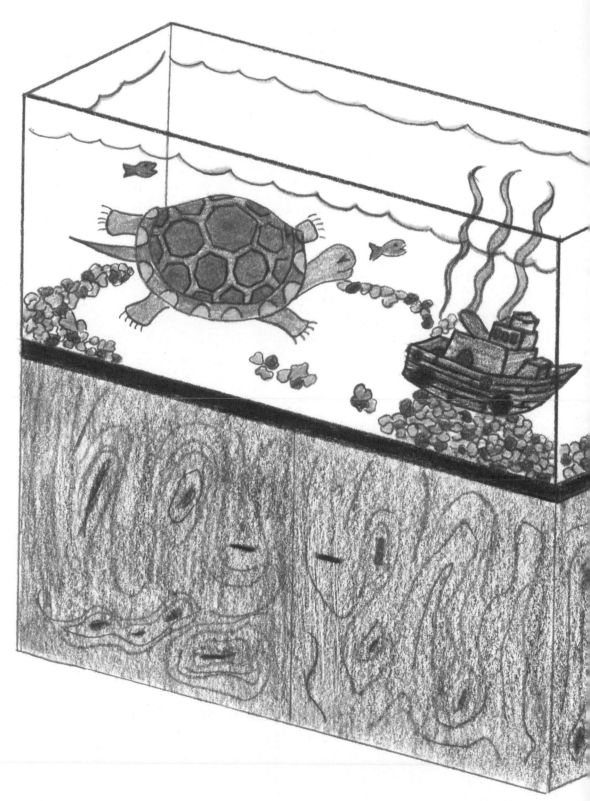

The minnows only last a day, and the one hundred grub worms are a snack for the enormous turtle. He is nearly three times the size of the biggest turtle in the pet store, and he looks like a giant sea turtle next to the miniature sandcastle in his tank.

On the weekend, the family piles into the car to go visit their favorite place at the local creek.

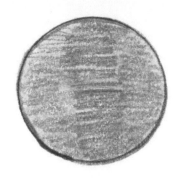

They load up their buckets, fish nets, and creek shoes to find Raphael more food. The sky is extremely bright.

The sunlight glistens upon the clear sparkling water and a rainbow appears with every splashing spree. Haley and Harold wade in the water.

Harold's pants are rolled up to his knees. They catch crayfish and minnows, and play in the water skipping stones, and splashing each other playfully.

"I wish I could find my own painted shell turtle," Haley sighs. "Then Harold and I would both have one."

"Painted shell turtles are a rare find in this area," says mom. "They look like rocks in the water, and they are the color of grass and moss. Maybe if you pray and ask God for a turtle, you will find one. God hears every one of your prayers."

Harold agrees. "Yeah! Raphael needs a friend so he's not lonely." Haley scouts the creek bed more diligently for the answer to her prayer,

a companion for Raphael,
her own pet turtle.

Playing at the creek is fun, but now, it is time to go. Harold is proud of his catch, but Haley is going home disappointed. She sits quietly peeking out the back-passenger window.

She pulls her tan fishing hat down over her eyes. Harold proudly watches his crayfish and minnows splash around in the bucket. He entertains himself all the way home by trying to get the crayfish to latch on to a stick.

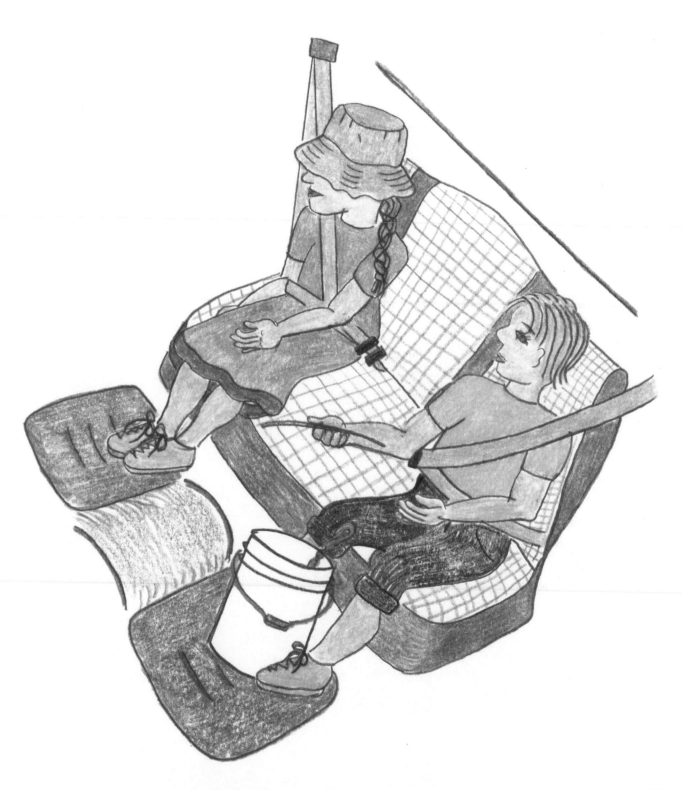

One month later, they return to their favorite creek. This time they take jojos and fried chicken for a picnic lunch. They unload the buckets, nets, and chicken and find places to sit on the stone bridge.

Haley plops down on the bridge with her legs crossed and eats her chicken dinner. After eating her last potato wedge, brushing the crumbs off her hands, she jumps up and shouts, "I see a turtle!"

"Where?!" asks Harold. He throws down his chicken and runs over to where Haley was sitting. Haley climbs down off the bridge and into the water. Harold argues. "That's a rock!"

"No, it's not! It's a turtle!" Haley squeals excitedly as she lifts the shiny green turtle out of the water.

The expression on her face is beaming like the sun. She smiles from ear to ear. "Mom, I found a turtle right in front of where I was sitting!"

"That's amazing! I would say that God answered that prayer, wouldn't you?"

"He sure did! It was right there in front of me the whole time I was eating." She put her turtle in the minnow bucket. "Now Raphael has a friend! I will name her Crystal."

"That's a good name. I would say that she is a crystal-clear answer to prayer, wouldn't you?" Mom winks and smiles.

"Yeah, she is." Haley smiles beautifully. This time the ride home is not so gloomy. Haley is proud of her rare find.

She has a new pet, some minnows and some crayfish, but the greatest treasure of the whole day is the answer to her prayer.

God heard her voice, and He answered her prayer!

Printed in the United States
by Baker & Taylor Publisher Services